Susan Anderson
Colorado's Doc Susie

Susan Anderson
Colorado's Doc Susie

A NOW YOU KNOW BIO

Number Fourteen in the Now You Know Bio® Series

Lydia Griffin

Filter Press, LLC
Palmer Lake, Colorado

To the Doc Susies in my life
D. Brown
T. Lerch
E. Stockwell
E. Thibodeau
O. Thibodeau

ISBN: 978-0-86541-108-1
Library of Congress Control Number: 2010936265
Copyright © 2010 by Lydia Griffin. All Rights Reserved.
Cover photography courtesy Colorado Historical Society, 10025815

No part of this publication may be reproduced or transmitted in any form or by any means, electronic or mechanical, including photocopy, audio recording, or any information storage and retrieval system, without permission in writing from the publisher.

Susan Anderson: Colorado's Doc Susie

Published by
Filter Press, LLC, P.O. Box 95, Palmer Lake, CO 80133
719-481-240
info@FilterPressBooks.com

Printed in the United States of America

Contents

1 Susie's Early Years 1
2 Susie's Education 7
3 Susie's Heartbreak 13
4 Becoming Doc Susie 19
5 Susie Finds a Home 26
6 Coroner Susie 35
7 Doctor of Grand County 42

Timeline 53
New Words 55
Sources 57
Index 59

Susan Anderson, January 31, 1870 – April 16, 1960
Susan had professional photographs taken when she graduated from medical school. She gave these pictures to friends and professors.

Doc Susie rushed through the swinging doors of Colorado General Hospital in Denver. She carried four-year-old Rudy in her strong arms. There was no time to waste. It had been a long ride through the mountains from Fraser, Colorado to Denver. Susie demanded that a surgeon remove Rudy's **appendix**. If it burst, he would die. A new doctor listened to the woman in shabby clothes. He explained that the little boy could be operated on only if a doctor had sent him to the hospital.

In the nick of time, Susie's friend, Dr. Meador, arrived. He introduced the young doctor to Susan Anderson, M.D. Dr. Meador said that Susie was one of Colorado's finest country physicians. "Doc Susie," he said, "has to find out what's wrong with a patient by putting her ear up to his chest in the dark in the midst of a blizzard, and [she] still gets it right."

That was the truth. In 1910, Doc Susie was the best doctor and the only doctor for miles around the mountain town of Fraser, Colorado.

1 Susie's Early Years

Susan Anderson was born on January 31, 1870, in Nevada Mills, Indiana, just north of Fort Wayne. She was the first of Marya Pile and William Henry Anderson's two children. Marya was originally from Louisiana. Susan did not look like her mother, who had straight black hair and dark eyes. Susan looked like her father. William also had roots in Louisiana. He had wavy brown hair and high cheekbones. Susan was a beautiful girl with a round face, high cheek-bones, and large eyes. Her light brown bangs dangled just above her eyebrows.

When Susan was two years old, her brother John was born. He had curly blonde hair and a lively personality. John liked to smile, and he made Susan laugh. They became very good friends as they got older.

In 1875, Susan's parents divorced. At that time, divorce was not as common as it is today. The divorce meant big changes for Susan and John. Within a year, Susan's father moved the family to a farm near Wichita, Kansas, far away from Indiana. Susan and John's grandparents, Aunt Lois, and Uncle John went, too. Susan's mother stayed in Indiana.

Kansas was very different from Indiana. The big shade trees and flowers that bloomed at home did not grow on the Kansas prairie. The wind blew tumbleweeds across the dirt roads. Susan didn't like Kansas. She and her brother missed Indiana and life with their mother.

Susan was named for her Grandmother Anderson. They were very close. Susan spent countless hours with her grandmother and with her Aunt Lois. From them, she learned how to do the work expected of a woman. Susan's grandmother taught her how to cook, crochet, and sew. Susan learned these skills, but she never enjoyed them. She preferred to be outdoors with her father. Together she and her father walked the busy streets of Wichita. On their farm, Susan watched him split wood and care for the animals. William taught Susan the ways of the Wild West. She learned to carry a gun, shoot rattlesnakes, and ride a horse.

Telegraph operators used a device like this to send Morse code messages. When the telegrapher pushed the bar down against a spring, it formed a circuit and allowed electricity to flow.

Susan also learned Morse code. She wanted to be a **telegrapher** when she grew up. Her father encouraged her to dream big. He wanted one of his children to be a doctor like his grandfather and great uncle had been.

Susan was very bright. She passed exams that allowed her to graduate from eighth grade at the one-room schoolhouse. Now she could attend high school in Wichita. But her father forced her to wait until John was ready for high school, too. William believed that Susan would keep her fun-loving brother in line, and they could **board** together in Wichita. Their farm was too far away from town to walk to and from school each day.

In the 1880s, anyone who had completed the eighth grade was allowed to teach grammar school. For two years, Susan taught reading, writing, and arithmetic while she waited for John. When the time came for John and Susan to go high school, William found a place for his children to live in downtown Wichita.

> ### Know More!
>
> **Telegrapher**
> Before the telephone and internet, the telegraph was used to communicate across long distances. The electrical telegraph was invented by Samuel F. B. Morse in 1837. The machine made it possible to send and receive messages in code. Morse and his partner, Alfred Vail, invented a special code they named Morse code. Morse code is an alphabet that represents letters with combinations of long and short sounds or light signals. Telegraphers used Morse code to send messages over the telegraph. During the American Civil War, many women became telegraphers because the men were away fighting the war. One of the most important roles of the telegrapher was to help keep trains safe and on schedule. Find a copy of the Morse code in a large dictionary or on line. Try writing your address in the code.

During their high school years, Susan and John spent most of their time together. John knew how to make his sister happy. He had a great sense of humor. Susan's relationship with John was very important to her. She told him everything. He was her best friend.

They studied English, Latin, algebra, geometry, physiology, geography, history, and physics. Susan did very well in school. John enjoyed a good time. When Susan was twenty-one and John nineteen, they graduated from high school. By now, Susan had changed

Susie's Early Years 5

Wichita High School, 1886. Susie and John Anderson graduated from the school in 1891.

her mind about the future. She no longer wished to be a telegrapher. She wanted to be a doctor.

While Susan and John were away at school in Wichita, their father met a young woman named Minnie. It had been more than fifteen years since Susan's parents had divorced. Minnie was only a few years older than Susan. Soon after Susan and John graduated from high school and returned to the farm, William and Minnie married. Susan and John hardly had time to adjust to these changes before more changes followed.

2 Susie's Education

Exciting news of easy riches was coming from the West. Gold had been discovered in the mountains of Colorado at a place called Cripple Creek. Susan's father saw an opportunity in Colorado. In 1892, he packed up his entire family again and headed west to join the gold rush. William did not have a very high opinion of miners. He never panned for gold himself. Instead, he set up businesses selling supplies to miners.

William settled his family in Barry, a small town one mile south of Cripple Creek in Squaw Gulch. Now, for the first time, Susan and John lived with Minnie. Minnie did not like Susan. She was jealous of Susan's relationship with William. Minnie went out of her way to make Susan's home life unhappy. After William and Minnie married, Susan and her father never had a close relationship again.

In 1893, Cripple Creek was a thriving town of more than 5,000 people. When the Andersons arrived, the town had four dance halls, seven bakeries, nine hotels, ten meat markets, eleven clothing stores, twenty-four grocery stores, six bookstores, and twenty-six saloons. It was also full of bad-tempered men, outlaws, and corruption. William didn't want Susan to be surrounded by such things. He encouraged her to follow her dream of becoming a doctor. In September 1893, Susan enrolled in medical school at the University of Michigan at Ann Arbor. She was glad that medical school was far away from Cripple Creek and Minnie.

At the same time, William decided that John should become a **civil engineer**. He shipped John off to school in Oakland, California.

Elizabeth Blackwell was the first woman in the United States to graduate from medical school. She earned her medical degree in 1849. She was a role model for other women who hoped to enter the profession. By 1897, when Susan started college in Ann Arbor, one in every four students was female. The work of a country physician was often called women's work. The daily tasks in a doctor's office included cleaning wounds, reducing fevers, and sterilizing instruments. These tasks were not attractive to many men.

Susan started medical school with only a high school diploma. She would receive her medical certification and her college degree at the same time. Learning came easily to her. Paying for school did not. It was expensive. In 1895, William Anderson's business was failing. Minnie grew nervous about their financial situation. She didn't want William to spend money on his older children because they were starting another family of their own. She convinced him to stop paying for Susan and John's education.

John surprised William by staying in California to continue his education. John took fewer classes so he could pay for them himself. He enjoyed the more relaxed schedule. John loved to play sports. He was an athlete. Once he rode a bicycle almost 500 miles, all the way from San Francisco to Los Angeles.

Susan also found a way to stay in school. A fellow student, Mary Lapham, offered to loan her money to finish her education. Mary was from a wealthy Michigan family. She started medical school but had to stop because she was ill with **tuberculosis**.

With Mary's help, Susan continued her studies. She

also had a job as an intern, or assistant doctor, at St. Catherine's Hospital. For months at a time, she worked at the hospital at night and attended classes during the day. She studied hard and was determined to become the best doctor she could be.

Susan grew angry with her father for not supporting her through school. He had changed since marrying Minnie. He was bossy and controlling. Susan missed

Know More!

Elizabeth Blackwell
Elizabeth Blackwell was the first woman doctor in the United States. She was born in England in 1821 and moved to the United States as a child. Elizabeth applied to many medical schools, but none would allow her to study because she was a woman. Geneva Medical College in New York asked the male students if they should accept her. Assuming it was a joke, the men said "yes," and so she began her studies there. She graduated from Geneva Medical College in 1849. She was number one in her class. She faced discrimination and hardship both studying and working in a field dominated by men.

She became a citizen of the United States but moved to Europe to continue studying and practicing medicine. Dr. Blackwell received additional training in Paris, and she dedicated her life to treating women and the poor. She died in 1910. Is your doctor a woman or a man? Do you think it makes a difference to patients? Visit a library to find out how many doctors are women today.

the relationship she used to have with her father and longed for her mother. Since Indiana was not far from Michigan, Susan decided to visit her.

In a letter to her brother written September 25, 1896, Susan told him about her visit with their mother:

> I went to mother's. She is a **queer** woman. She is very quiet and seems so sad and brokenhearted. I stayed only a little while for it was too **melancholy** and sad to stay long. She has four other children…They all made a great fuss over me and I know I was welcome. She [mother] gave me some pieces of her dresses, a roll for each of us. She has your first pants and gave me a small piece, I'll send you part.

Her mother had remarried a man named William McLaughlin and started a new family. They had two young children of their own, Cuba and Louis. Susan felt that her mother's life no longer included her older children. The visit did not give Susan the great comfort she hoped for. Though she and Marya continued to write letters, it was the last time she ever saw her mother.

In the spring of 1897, Susan received an offer to work at the Women's Hospital of Philadelphia. She looked forward to the challenge. However, she was not well. She had developed a **chronic** cough during her last semester of medical school. One of her professors noticed that her cough continued to get worse. He suggested she return to Cripple Creek. Doctors often sent patients with **respiratory** diseases to Colorado because the higher altitude and dry air was good for the lungs. Susan realized she had developed tuberculosis. If she didn't listen to her professor, she had little chance of getting better.

Know More!

Tuberculosis

Tuberculosis, or TB, is a bacterial infection of the lungs, but it can spread to other organs. Most people get tuberculosis by breathing air that has been infected by a person with the disease who has sneezed or coughed.

Symptoms of TB include coughing, wheezing, fever, fatigue, and chest pain. Before there were medicines for treating TB, many people with TB were sent to live in sanatoriums. Sanatoriums were large medical facilities where patients could be kept away from the general public. Rest, nutrition, and light exercise were thought to be the best remedies for TB. Though many people recovered from tuberculosis, the disease often led to death.

3 Susie's Heartbreak

Susan left Michigan in the summer of 1897. For three years, she lived in the mining town of Anaconda, near Cripple Creek. She arrived in the Cripple Creek area one year after a fire had destroyed most of the town's businesses.

More than $2 million worth of property had gone up in flames. The blaze started in the Portland Hotel. Outlaws who planned to rob the First National Bank probably started the fire to create a **distraction**. Thousands of people were left homeless. By the time Susan arrived, the residents of Cripple Creek had rebuilt their homes and businesses. Cripple Creek was booming once again.

Susan set up a small medical practice. It was located on the Bi-Metallic Block, near the famous Bi-Metallic Bank in Cripple Creek. Susan wrote John, who was still in California, to ask his business advice. On July 12, 1897, he replied:

> You asked for advice. Any fool can give advice and I am no exception to the rule. Never the less perhaps I can make some helpful suggestions.
> Of course you should have a sign printed or rather painted in an attractive way. Next, you should have some cards printed. The Dr's code of rules perhaps you know if not learn it. If I were you I would try to make your contemporary Dr's your friends anyway not your enemies, Be as cheerful and entertaining as possible when with your patients. This you will find "takes." One thing more for yourself. Do not get cast down, "Rome was not built in a day" neither will a practice be.

When Susan opened her medical office in Cripple Creek, there were 55 doctors serving a population of 30,000. There was one doctor for every 500 people. Susan was busy. By 1899, she had repaid her loan to Mary Lapham. Susan was finding success as a doctor, but her relationship with her father and Minnie made living in the same town difficult.

Susan and John wrote many letters back and forth, often about their family. In one letter, Susan wrote:

> Pa has ruined one woman's life by his trifling or haste or change of heart or something and she is our mother…it makes me feel hard and bitter and sour when I have to go in old shabby clothes and scrimp and save and board off Grandma and Grandpa & Minnie gets new things for her and the babies and goes to all expense she needs and grumbles about not being able to treat me as she likes to on account of Pa and I know Pa would be glad to have things different and comfortable.

In a more encouraging letter dated September 2, 1899, Susan wrote:

> You know I always said if we (you and I) excelled in anything in particular it was sticking to it, and though it has been a pretty hard pull sometimes and looked "kind of **dubious**" still we are alive and coming up yet. Pa may point us out as his son and his daughter but he can't say he ever did much for either of us that we wouldn't

have done without him for we neither one would be kept down with "common kids." Of course that wouldn't do to tell people outside.

The twentieth century started out promising for Susan. In 1900, she was delighted when John returned to Colorado to help with the family business. Now she had her brother close by.

She was also excited because her dream of getting married and having a family of her own was about to

Susan and her father, William Anderson.
The young man is probably Susan's brother, John.

come true. She had plans to marry the love of her life.

Then, in March 1900, everything changed for the worse. Without warning or explanation, the man she loved, W. R. left her. He moved away. Susan suspected her father had something to do with W. R. disappearing. Whatever the reason was, Susan's heart was broken. She wrote, "Don't trust **two faced** people with any affair that involves the happiness of your life and the life that should be dearest and most protected by you."

On March 16, Susan's heart broke again. Her brother John had been sick with pneumonia. Nobody had told Susan. By the time she arrived to help, it was too late. Susan wrote in her journal about the sad days that surrounded John's death:

> **Sunday March 11, 1900:** John sick with pneumonia. **Monday March 12, 1900:** Pictures returned from W. R., the end of a vain hope. No use to cast pearls before swine.

Susan's journals explain how she felt at the time. She had hoped that W. R. might change his mind if he saw pictures. Maybe he would come back. He didn't. Susan compared offering her love to W.R. to offering pearls to a pig. What is the point of that? Pigs don't care about jewelry.

She continued:

> **Friday March 16, 1900:** John died at 6:15 p.m. Was so strange to think of John dead but he has suffered all **mortal** can. We are happy he died **unconscious** of his pain. **Saturday March 17, 1900:** Went to see John. Poor baby he is so sweet at rest. **Sunday March 18, 1900:** Saw John. Selected casket of black with silk cords. **Monday March 19, 1900:** John buried today. He is gone from sight but is not far away. I seem to feel that he is near me and knows all the troubles and how I feel. **Tuesday March 20, 1900:** Come back to Cripple Creek to live again. Life seems so useless and in vain. No one now cares much whether I live or die. John was my best friend on earth and now my best friend is in heaven.

4 Becoming Doc Susie

After so much sadness, Susan needed a change. She took a job as the private doctor for a rich man. He was ill but liked to travel. Traveling with him she saw cities in the eastern United States and in Canada. Soon the man was well enough to journey overseas. Susan did not want to go along. She returned to Colorado and set up a medical practice in Denver.

Unfortunately, her practice failed. She later explained in a newspaper interview: "[The failure was] because people just didn't believe in women doctors."

In fall of 1901, Susan moved to Greeley, Colorado, a ranching and farming community north of Denver. She accepted a job as a nurse. It was the only work she could find. But she did not like taking orders from men. She often knew more than they did.

She considered moving. At one point, she traveled to Steamboat Springs where she thought she might settle. In the end, she decided that Steamboat Springs was too remote. She would have to stay in Greeley until she found a better location.

Susan cleaned wounds and emptied bedpans for years. She coughed a lot and felt tired. She finally realized that she was sick with tuberculosis again. If she didn't move to a higher elevation, the disease would get worse.

When Susan was almost thirty-eight years old, she bundled herself in a woolen coat and fur hat and traveled to the small mountain town of Fraser, Colorado. She intended to make it her home. Fraser was located high in the Rocky Mountains. She had visited Fraser earlier in the fall, when the aspen leaves changed from vibrant green to brilliant yellow. Fraser was a quiet town with only a few residents. She decided it was the perfect place for her. She arrived to stay in Fraser in December 1907.

The little town was just off the tracks of the Denver Northwestern and Pacific Railway, otherwise known as the Moffat Road. The only way to get to her new home was to take the train up and over Rollins Pass, the steep and narrow road up and over the mountains. The

Moffat Road had been completed in June 1904. It was the highest railroad line in North America.

Snow buried the train tracks in the winter. Wind gusts reached 100 miles per hour. There was always a risk of an **avalanche**. Susan was willing to take the risks. She was confident in the railroad crew headed by conductor George Barnes. She was grateful they kept the train running in the winter.

Susan didn't travel to Fraser alone. She had a little white dog with her. He had long, fluffy, white fur. His tail curled up over his back. Susan's dog didn't look like he would do well in the harsh climate of Fraser. Surprisingly, he did. She took him everywhere she went.

Susan focused on her health when she first arrived in town. She prescribed herself a routine of exercise and rest to help her weak lungs. She did not tell anyone she was a doctor. At that time, there were only eleven homes in the community. Men came from all over the world to work at the lumber camps and sawmills just outside of town.

After several months of **recuperation** and exercise, Susan felt better. Her new friends, Cora and Charlie Warner, hired her to work in their general store. Lumberjacks came into town frequently. There was not

Doc Susie traveled to the lumber camps and sawmills in Middle Park. Most of the workers at the camps were men, but they often brought their families to live with them. In this photograph, a little girl stands with her father.

much work for them when the snow melted leaving lots of mud. Cowboys and ranchers returned to Fraser after spending winters at lower elevations.

Susan still dreamed of having a family of her own one day. There were plenty of men in the area. It seemed a sure thing that she would find a partner. To her, a life without children seemed depressing and wasteful. Susan hated to waste and continued to wait for love. In Fraser, she was called "Susie". The nickname suited her.

Susie enjoyed work at the Warner's store. It was an opportunity for her to meet the townspeople and perhaps a husband.

One spring day in 1908, a cowboy barged into the store. He hollered for a doctor. Susie offered to help. He explained that "Dave" had been cut on barbed wire. She grabbed her black bag and followed the young man to a barn. She assumed his friend Dave was resting in the barn. When she walked into the barn, she gasped. Dave was not the cowboy's friend. He was his horse.

Susie worked carefully stitching Dave's cuts. Later she recalled, "Every time I stitched up that wound, the horse yanked the stitches out with his teeth, but I pulled him through." Before long, the news spread. There was a new lady doctor in town. By 1909, Susie's career as a **rural** physician was established. It was not uncommon for doctors to double as veterinarians. Doc Susie, as she liked to be called, continued to treat animals occasionally. She had to tolerate a lot of **skepticism** from the local men. But the women loved having a female doctor in town. It was her compassionate and understanding temperament that kept her in business.

One of her first patients was a baby girl, not yet one-year-old. The baby's parents lived in Arrow, a lumber camp outside of Fraser. Doc Susie caught a ride on a **freight train** to get to the camp. When she arrived, the baby was cuddled in her mother's arms. The parents were from Sweden and did not speak English. A translator helped her communicate with the family. Doc Susie often needed a translator, as many of her patients did not speak English.

Doc Susie discovered that the baby suffered from scurvy. Scurvy is a bone disease that comes from not getting enough vitamins. When Doc Susie asked what the baby ate, the mother said that she fed her canned milk. Doc Susie explained that milk from cans did not have the nutrients infants needed. They needed the milk from women, cows, or goats. Doc Susie knew that the baby would probably die.

The mother and father did not know that they had been doing anything wrong. At the logging camp, there were few comforts and no pennies to spare. Doc Susie learned that most babies were delivered without a doctor. The workers could not afford one. Doc Susie demanded that they send for her the next time they had an illness or emergency. She didn't care if they couldn't afford to pay her. She only wanted to help.

Helping sick people was Doc Susie's philosophy. She

taught the benefits of good nutrition to her friends and patients. She talked about vitamins and minerals. She believed that if a person ate well and exercised, many diseases and infections could be avoided.

Many of Doc Susie's patients could not pay her the 25 cents she charged for house calls. It was too much money for them. So, instead of money, her patients paid her with firewood for her stove, or by asking her to dinner and baking her pies. Eventually, she was paid with a house.

5 Susie Finds a Home

When Susie first moved to town, she rented a shack near the railroad tracks. The Moffat Road had been built with the money of a powerful Denver businessman named David Moffat. He wanted to find an affordable way to carry freight in and out of Denver. It was the only way to compete with other booming cities like Cheyenne, Wyoming. The Moffat Road was part of the answer.

In 1913, the railroad changed names to the Denver and Salt Lake Railroad. Though everyone still called it the Moffat Road. One day, the railroad general manager, Bill Freeman, knocked on the door of Doc Susie's shack. He told her that her cabin sat on a railroad **right-of-way**, and she would have to move. Even though she was a busy doctor, she made little money. Few patients paid her for the treatment she gave. Susie was as poor as her patients. She could not afford to rent or buy a new house. The railroad offered to help pay for her move. But where was she going to go?

Susie often thought of her childhood home in Indiana. She remembered the mild winters, spring rains, hot summers, and beautiful fall foliage. She had a passion for roses, and she dreamed of returning to Indiana where she could grow a garden of roses. Now that she was forced to move, she considered Indiana. But Doc Susie couldn't leave the responsibilities she had in Fraser. People depended on her.

Susie was 43 years old. She had given up on the dream of having children. The people of **Middle Park** were her family, and they valued her. A hay rancher gave her a log storage barn. It was payment for a medical bill

Know More!

Middle Park

A park is a large open space. The Middle Park of Colorado is a valley located in Grand County. The towns of Fraser, Granby, Grand Lake, Winter Park, Tabernash, Radium, Hot Sulphur Springs, and Kremmling are all in Middle Park. Find North Park, South Park, and Middle Park on a Colorado map. Can you locate parks in other western states?

Many of Doc Susie's patients could not afford to pay her with money. Instead, they paid her by doing things for her or by giving her things she could use, such as firewood. In 1913, she was paid with a four-room house. Glass from an old car was used as a window in the front door. Her house did not have a foundation. This 2009 photograph shows how crooked the windows became over the years without a foundation to support the house.

he owed her. She would have to move it, log by log, but it was hers for the taking.

Two men who worked at the sawmill heard the news of her **eviction**. The men showed her a vacant lot that could be hers for the low price of one dollar. Exchanging money, even just one dollar, made the sale official. The men also offered to help move the logs. Other men from the lumber camp helped build the house. They also put on a new roof. Doc Susie had a home again.

The new house was just a block and a half from the railroad tracks. It was a great location, she said. She could still hear the rumble of the locomotives and the whistle of an approaching train. The house had a steep roof, so the snow would slide off. She didn't want to shovel her roof in the winter. With a wood stove for heat and a well in the yard, she lived without indoor plumbing and electricity. When her father learned of Susie's new house, he sent her a special clock that only had to be wound every eight days.

She had a telephone in her old shack. In this home, she chose not to have it installed. Doc Susie didn't like using a telephone. Now, her patients would have to send someone to fetch her in person.

Life was very busy. Though Susie had a room in her new home for examining patients, she continued to make house calls most of the time. She traveled from one side of Middle Park to the other to treat the sick. Sometimes she would walk four miles to the town of Tabernash or climb a 13,000–foot peak in order to get to injured timber workers. One family even trusted her enough to take their four-year-old son, Rudy, on a train to Denver to have his appendix removed. According to journalist Eugene Foster:

She has used every type of **conveyance**—sleigh, skis, snowshoes, horses, and the automobile—for her missions of mercy through the mountains with temperatures as low as 50 degrees below zero and raging blizzards.

Doc Susie said, "[It would snow] so hard I couldn't see the horses in front of the sleigh."

Susie felt safe carrying a gun and a cowbell. She whistled and sang songs on her long walks to reach patients. For a time, her favorite song was "Oh! What a Beautiful Morning." Patients could hear her shouting the lyrics before she arrived at their home.

Doc Susie dressed for the cold weather by layering petticoats and woolen undergarments. She wore felt boots with rubber galoshes over them to keep her feet dry. She never wore a **corset** except for the time she broke several ribs. She wore the corset to help hold her broken ribs in place so they would heal. No matter where Doc Susie traveled, she dressed like a lady. She never wore pants. When she climbed over something or onto a horse, she asked the men to look away.

In June 1914, a war broke out thousands of miles away. World War I would bring changes to Fraser. The war immediately increased the need for fuel. The Moffat Road was busier than ever hauling coal from the nearby Yampa coal fields. Coal trains had to go over Rollins Pass to deliver the fuel to Denver.

Snow on the tracks was always a problem. Trains with snowplows attached to the front attempted to plow through the packed snow. This required a lot of power from the mallet locomotives. Mallets were designed for travel on steep mountain tracks. They were

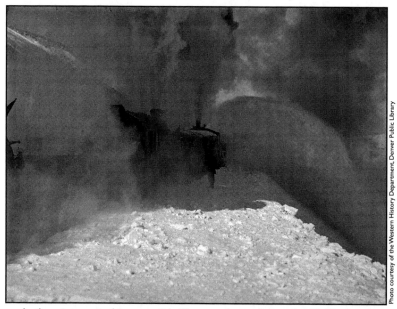

In the winter months, snow slid off mountains and onto the Moffat Road. In order to pass through, snowplow trains were used. Snowplow trains were powered by the Mallet. It was very expensive to keep the railroad free of snow. It was also dangerous.

The Yampa coal fields were located 85 miles from Fraser in Routt County. The coal fields covered almost 900 square miles and held over five billion tons of extractable coal. Miners worked underground in cold, dark conditions.

slow and steady, with two engines that carried heavy weight. Mallets were expensive to run and maintain. Almost half of the money the railroad made was spent on managing the snow on the tracks. A tunnel through James Peak was the answer, but the railroad company had no money to build one. Fraser residents worried the railroad would go out of business. Without the railroad, the town would face hard times.

To distract themselves from their worries, the town's residents held parties. Doc Susie's friends threw "Hard

The Mallet is a steam-powered, compound engine locomotive. They are smaller than other locomotives and designed for small, narrow railways. Mallets are powerful and useful for hauling heavy loads. Mallets were used on the Moffat Road to help plow snow from Rollins Pass.

Times" themed parties. Everyone dressed as a hobo and drank from tin cans. Local musicians strummed guitars and played fiddles. Dancers used the center of the barn as the dance floor. For one party, Doc Susie wore a flour sack. Written across the back was the flour brand name, Pride of the Rockies. The name fit her well. She was the pride of Fraser.

The Great Influenza **Epidemic** of 1918 followed the end of World War I. The epidemic claimed the lives of many Middle Park residents. Poverty, harsh living conditions, and bodies strained from hard labor meant the epidemic hit Fraser especially hard. Doc Susie did not get much rest. She treated influenza, or flu, patients as she would treat someone with pneumonia. She tried to bring down their high fevers by soaking patients in a lukewarm bath. She also gave them one of her special blue pills to lessen the symptoms. Though no one knew what was in the special pills, longtime Fraser residents guess it was a vitamin. Doc Susie had always believed in good nutrition and **preventive medicine.**

Doc Susie was unable to save most of the influenza victims. Losing a patient was as hard for Susie as it was for any other doctor. In this small community, she considered her patients her friends, too.

6 Coroner Susie

By the end of the war, talk of building a tunnel for the railroad was heard in every mountain community along the tracks. The bad economy affected most everyone in Colorado. If the train had not had to chug over Rollins Pass, it would have been profitable during the war. Something needed to change.

On April 29, 1922, the Moffat Tunnel Improvement District started preparing to build a tunnel. It would be a big job. Tunneling through rocky mountains would take several years. This would be the longest tunnel in the entire United States.

Building the tunnel would not be easy. It would be a dangerous undertaking. In 1926, Grand County Sheriff Mark Fletcher asked Susie to serve as **coroner** during the construction. It was important to have a doctor who would tell the truth about the accidents that killed workers. Doc Susie was nervous about being the doctor who would investigate the cause of deaths. She liked to help the living. But it was important work, and she was poor and could not afford to say no.

During her years as coroner, Susie developed strong opinions about the tunnel construction. She didn't approve of the way the tunnel was dug. One crew blasted and dug from the east side of the mountain, the East Portal. Another crew did the same from the west side, or the West Portal. The plan was for the crews to blast through the mountain until they reached each other. Susie was always on duty.

The most devastating call came when a portion of the tunnel caved in at the West Portal. Dr. Roderick J. McDonald, who was in charge of the hospital at the West Portal, attempted to save one man who had been rescued. Five other men remained trapped inside. Word of the cave-in spread quickly. The *Rocky Mountain News* and the *Denver Post* sent reporters to the scene. The reporters tried to get the names of the victims and the details of the story. But Doc Susie wanted what was right for the suffering men, which was privacy.

Finally, the cave-in area was cleaned up. The bodies of the men were located. Sheriff Fletcher asked Susie

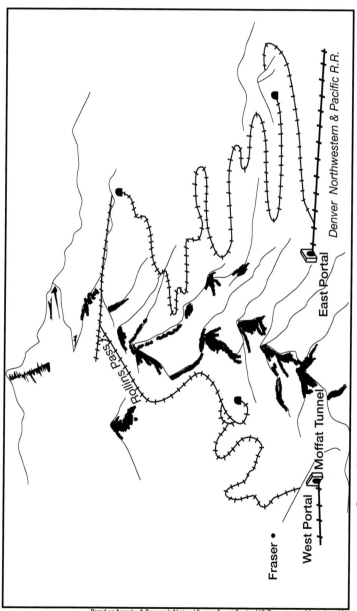

Route of the original Denver Northwestern and Pacific Railway over Rollins Pass. The new route through the Moffat Tunnel was shorter, safer, and less expensive.

Based on Arapaho & Roosevelt National Forests Forest Service U.S. Department of Agriculture Map if she would go into the tunnel to pronounce the men dead. She was surprised when the reporters went into the tunnel with her. They rode into the tunnel in a small tram car. It was quiet, dark, and dank. She examined the bodies of the five men to identify the exact cause of death. She also had to remove the valuables from their pockets. Later, she would try to return the belongings to their families.

A day later, articles about the cave-in were printed in the newspapers. Susie was disgusted by the reporters' descriptions and dramatic explanations. She had not viewed the scene the same way they had. She believed they had **embellished** their stories.

During the decade that Susie served as the coroner, her frustration with the newspapers grew. Reporters saw things differently than she did. This made Doc Susie upset. Newspapers continuously reported on accidental deaths at the tunnel. Susie knew that even more men were dying from work-related problems. The cruel conditions of digging through a mountain caused men to suffer loss of eyesight, pneumonia, chronic coughs, and infections.

The victims of the tunnel construction were the men Susie had once known as lumberjacks. They were the hard workers from the sawmills. The lumberjacks took jobs in the tunnel because the lumber business was in decline. The forests had been cleared, and there was not much timber left to cut. The tunnel project gave work to many former lumberjacks.

Susie looked forward to the shorter and safer route that the tunnel would provide for the trains. But she knew better than most people. The tunnel came at great expense. It not only cost money, it also cost lives.

The Moffat Tunnel made travel through the mountains easier. Trains no longer had to climb up and over Rollins Pass. The Moffat Tunnel was six miles long and cost $18 million to build. It was completed on February 26, 1928. This photograph shows the entrance at the East Portal.

On February 12, 1927, the east and west portal crews met. The tunnel was dug through. It was six miles long and cost nearly $18 million to build. One year later, on February 26, 1928, the first train chugged through the Moffat Tunnel. Everyone in Middle Park was invited to a special ribbon-cutting ceremony at the East Portal. But no one was allowed to walk in the tunnel before the first train came through. That meant the residents of Fraser were not allowed to take the shortcut through the tunnel. They would have to take the night train over Rollins Pass and then wait a long time in the cold weather for the ceremony to begin. They chose not to do this.

Instead, local residents watched the first trains popped out from the tunnel at the West Portal. The train was packed full of paying customers and official guests. Bill Freeman, the man who had evicted Susie from her shack years earlier, was on board. Susie wanted everyone to know who built the tunnel. She was annoyed that the *Denver Post* made such a big deal over the celebration. She used a broom dipped in tar to make a cardboard sign. She wrote, "WE BUILT THE TUNNEL. THE POST DIDN'T." As the train poked through the West Portal, all the passengers saw the sign.

The superintendent of the railroad ordered that the sign be taken down. It was twenty years before word got out that the sign had been Doc Susie's idea.

7 Doctor of Grand County

Work slowed down for Doc Susie after the tunnel opened. She did not have to worry about the frequent injuries from the tunnel dig, and the lumber camps were almost all closed. The gold rush and the mining industry had dried up. She just took care of sick Fraser residents now.

In the early 1930s, the United States experienced years of little economic growth and widespread unemployment called the Great Depression. One in every four Americans did not have a job. The entire country was affected. However, Doc Susie's life changed little. She continued to have a hard time collecting fees from her patients. The money she did make, she hid in her house. Doc Susie did not trust banks.

Times were hard. Around 1932, Doc Susie decided to move back to Indiana. She packed all of her belongings in crates. Local resident Mildred Thompson said, "I am sure the crates were probably worth more than the contents but it was all important to her." She loaded up a boxcar and traveled by train east to Indiana. The residents of Fraser wondered what life would be like without Doc Susie.

They did not have to wonder for long. Within a few weeks, she was back. The Indiana she remembered so fondly was gone. "The only thing she ever said to me

Know More!

The Great Depression

The Great Depression was a time in America when many people struggled to pay for the necessities of life. On October 29, 1929, the stock market crashed. This meant that people lost the money they had invested. Soon, American businesses and banks closed, and employees lost their jobs. One in four workers did not have a job to go to. The crisis in America affected other countries as well.

In 1932, Franklin Delano Roosevelt was elected president. He attempted to strengthen the economy with government programs. His efforts helped to reduce the unemployment rate to 15 percent. But it wasn't until 1939 that the American economy began to recover. World War II was going on in Europe. Governments there needed supplies and ammunition that factories and businesses in the United States could make. People returned to work, and the Great Depression ended.

about it was that she hadn't been accepted," said Mildred Thompson. No one knows if Susie ever completely unpacked after she returned to Fraser. Many residents say that she continued to live out of boxes for the rest of her life.

On December 7, 1941, the Japanese bombed Pearl Harbor in Hawaii. The United States entered World War II, which was already going on in Europe. Doc Susie was very patriotic. She believed that supporting the troops and the country was important. She always paid a visit to the Middle Park mothers whose sons were soldiers.

Once, Doc Susie treated a sailor passing through on the train. He had punched his fist through a glass window. Doc Susie was happy to treat a man whom she considered a hero. He was so grateful for her fine care that his mother in New York sent a handmade blanket to Susie to thank her.

In 1942, Doc Susie remained Fraser's only physician. She was 72 years old. She had grown accustomed to her lonely lifestyle. She had never married nor had children. In 1951, she told Eugene Foster, "I could have [married] if I hadn't flown off the handle so much and said 'pooh' too many times."

After Winter Park Ski Area opened in 1939, Doc Susie was frequently called to set bones or help with other ski injuries. If she was not tending to a patient, she spent most of her days wandering around town. Sometimes, she picked through neighborhood trash. Because she was often paid for her services in firewood, she did had money to buy only the things she needed. She bought only the bare necessities. Sometimes she did not even buy food.

Winter Park Ski Resort opened in December 1939, a few miles from Fraser. Lift tickets cost one dollar, and there was one rope tow. Doc Susie treated injured skiers during the winter.

Susie never liked to cook. She preferred to visit her neighbors around dinnertime. They always invited her to join them. Mildred Thompson remembers feeling upset when Susie stopped by for supper. "I was young and **ignorant**," Mildred said. "It makes me feel just terrible that it took me so many years to appreciate her worth."

In 1947, Doc Susie returned to Michigan to attend the 50th anniversary of her graduation from medical school. She was 77 years old. Doc Susie is on the right.

Doc Susie was an exceptional woman. She was honored by the University of Michigan in 1947, fifty years after graduating from the school. They recognized her contribution to rural medicine. Eugene Foster wrote about talking to Doc Susie about the award. "Gazing thoughtfully toward the tree-dotted mountainside and gently rubbing the gold 'emeritus' pin, she [Doc Susie] whispered, 'just 50 years of good hard work.'"

Susie could have made money at one point in her life. A *Pic* magazine article written about her in the 1950s caused Ethel Barrymore to ask Susie if she could make a movie of her life. Barrymore was a famous actress and the great aunt of Drew Barrymore, who is a well-known actress today. Doc Susie turned her down with one word, "Fiddlesticks!" It was one of her favorite expressions.

As Doc Susie aged, was easily spotted in the small town. She continued to wear long skirts with long underwear underneath, even though fashion had changed. Her hair was long and white. She always wore it pinned neatly into a bun. She was a confident elderly woman who said what was on her mind. Edith Johnson Henson writes, "Nothing escaped her criticism—if she thought your dress was too short or you had too much make-up on, she didn't hesitate to tell you…you might say that she was the **conscience** of Fraser."

Doc Susie lived by the saying, "Waste not, want

not." She hated to throw anything anyway. By the time she was in her 80s, her house was a cluttered mess. To get around her living room, she created narrow paths through the stacks of books, newspapers, and catalogs.

Doc Susie loved to read. She particularly enjoyed reading the Bible. She memorized passages and often recited them to her patients.

Doc Susie practiced medicine until she was 84 years old. She continued to travel to patients in need, bundled in a sheep's wool coat with a scarf tied tightly around her hat, and she always carried her gun. Though she suffered from **arthritis**, she treated anyone in need.

Only once or twice did she bring a patient to her home for treatment. She was originally going to use one of her four rooms as an examining room. However, she never kept the house clean enough to actually see patients. Even though she cleaned wounds so carefully that no one ever got an infection, she did not care for housework. She became even more careless in her housekeeping as she grew older.

By 1956, Doc Susie had suffered a series of **strokes** and could no longer live alone. On October 27 of that year, she moved to the Samaritan Ltd. Nursing Home on Pennsylvania Street in Denver. With no family and

Doc Susie left Frasier in 1956. She had been the area's doctor for 47 years.

no money, it is unclear who paid for her to live there. Susie was so well-respected by doctors in Denver, it is possible that they arranged payment for her care.

Doc Susie passed away on April 16, 1960, at the age of 90. She died without a penny to her name. She wanted to be buried near her brother in the family's burial plot. But by the time she passed away, the Mt. Pisgah Graveyard in Cripple Creek was overgrown. No one could locate John's grave. She was buried in an unmarked grave. Grand County residents learned of this and took up a collection for their friend and longtime doctor. With the money raised, they had a headstone etched with her birth date, the date she died, and the words "Doctor of Grand County 1909-1956."

When Doc Susie moved to Fraser there were only eleven homes. Today Fraser has almost one thousand residents. The elevation is 8,574 feet above sea level.

In 1991, Virginia Cornell wrote an adult biography of Doc Susie titled *Doc Susie: The True Story of a Country Physician in the Colorado Rockies*. Her book has created a lasting legacy in Colorado of the famous country doctor. The author said that she felt indebted to Doc Susie and wanted to do something to honor her. "What do you do for a dead woman?" she wondered.

Virginia Cornell located the family plot in the Mt. Pisgah Graveyard. She hired a stone carver to carve Doc Susie's name where Susie had hoped to be remembered, next to her brother. Cornell's gift could not have been more perfect. She made Doc Susie's final wish come true.

The Denver and Rio Grande railroad still chugs through Fraser.

Timeline

1870 – Susan Anderson is born in Indiana.

1872 – Susan's brother, John, is born.

1875 – Susan's parents divorce.

1876 – William Anderson moves the family to Kansas.

1876 – Colorado becomes a state.

Alexander Graham Bell invents the telephone.

1890 – Gold is discovered in Cripple Creek, Colorado.

1891 – Susan and John graduate from high school.

William Anderson remarries.

1892 – Anderson family moves to Colorado.

1893 – Susan starts medical school at the University of Michigan in Ann Arbor.

1897 – Susan graduates from medical school and begins a medical practice in Cripple Creek.

1900 – Susan's fiancé leaves her and John dies of pneumonia.

1901 – Susan moves to Denver to start a practice. When it fails, she moves to Greeley, Colorado.

1904 – The Moffat Road opens.

1907 – Susan moves to Fraser.

1909 – Susan begins her practice in Fraser.

1914 – World War I begins in Europe.

1918 – World War I ends. The Great Influenza Epidemic kills more people than the war.

1920 – The 19th Amendment to the Constitution gives women the right to vote.

1922 – The Moffat Tunnel Improvement District is created.

1926 – Doc Susie is appointed coroner of Grand County.

1928 – The Moffat Tunnel opens.

1929 – The stock market crashes; the Great Depression begins.

1932 – Susie moves to Indiana but soon returns to Fraser.

1935 – The Great Depression recovery begins.

1939 – Winter Park Ski Resort opens.

1941 – The Japanese bomb Pearl Harbor and the United States enters World War II.

1945 – World War II ends.

1956 – Doc Susie moves to a nursing home in Denver.

1960 – Doc Susie dies at age 90.

New Words

appendix – a small piece of tissue attached to the large intestine

arthritis – a painful condition involving damage to the joints of the body

avalanche – a mass of snow or ice tumbling rapidly down a mountain

board – to receive lodging and meals in exchange for payment or services

chronic – a condition or disease that continues for a long time

civil engineer – a person who designs and builds bridges, roads, and dams

conscience – a knowledge of what is right and wrong together with a sense of duty to do what is right

conveyance – a way to move about or get around

coroner – an official who finds out the causes of deaths, especially ones believed to be violent or accidental

corset – a tight fitting undergarment worn for support

dubious – doubtful, questionable, or unlikely

embellished – added false details to a story in order to create interest

epidemic – a widespread disease that makes many people ill at the same time

eviction – a process of forcing someone to leave a rented home or property

freight train – a group of railroad cars pulled by one or more locomotives to move goods or cargo

ignorant – unknowing, unaware, uneducated

melancholy – depressed, unhappy, gloomy

preventive – seeking to avoid, or prevent, illness or disease

queer – strange, odd

respiratory disease – an illness affecting the lungs and breathing system

recuperation – recovery from illness

right-of-way – a legal right to use a certain route over someone's land

rural – having to do with the countryside

skepticism – doubtfulness, disbelief, criticism

stroke – a disturbance in the blood supply to the brain that can quickly cause damage

tuberculosis – an infection in the lungs that can lead to death

two-faced – deceitful or not sincere

Sources

Anderson, John. Personal Letters to Susan. Grand County Historical Museum archives.

Anderson, Susan. Personal diary. March 11-20, 1900.

Anderson, Susan. Letters to her brother John. Grand County Historical Museum archives.

Baumgarten, Idelia D. *Pioneer Personalities: Dr. Susan Anderson.* Ts. 5 January 1980.

Black, Robert C. III. *Island in the Rockies: The Pioneer Era of Grand County, Colorado.* Granby, CO: Grand County Pioneer Society, 1969.

Bollinger, Edward T. *Rails That Climb.* Golden, CO: Colorado Railroad Museum, 1979.

Bonnifield, Paul. Personal Interview. 1 August 2010.

Brady, Roger. Letters to Virginia Cornell. Grand County Historical Museum archives.

Cornell, Virginia. *Doc Susie: The True Story of a Country Physician in the Colorado Rockies.* New York: Ballantine, 1991.

Cornell, Virginia. Personal Interview. 12 November 2009k.

"Death Comes to 'Doc Susie'" *Denver Post.* 21 April 1960.

"Dr. Susan Anderson, Lady Doctor." *Grand County Historical Association Journal.* Volume XIV, Number 1.

"Dr. Anderson Maker Her Calls." Unidentifiable magazine. Colorado Historical Society.

Frank, Margery. "Doc Susie." Unidentified magazine. *11 May 1943.*

"Fraser's Pioneer 'Doc Susie' Dies at 90." *Rocky Mountain News.* 21 April 1960.

Foster, Eugene. "Pioneer Medic, 'Doc Susie' Still Going Strong at 81." Unidentifiable newspaper. Colorado Historical Society.

"A Guided Walking Tour of Beautiful Fraser, Colorado." Doc Susie's house. Autumn 2003.

Henson, Edith Johnson. Letter to Virginia Cornell. Grand County Historical Museum archives.

Jamison, Darlene, ed. Ts. Doc Susie Evening. Personal Memories from locals. 30 March 1977.

Jones, Rebecca. "The real Dr. Quinn from Colorado?" *Rocky Mountain News.* 2 January 1998.

Lakes, Arthur. "The Yampa Coal Fields: A Description of the Anthracite, Bituminous, and Lignite Field Traversed by the Moffat Road in Routt County, Colorado." *Mine and Minerals.* Vol XXIV—No. 6. January 1904.

"Lore, Legend, and Fact…Doc Susie—High Country Physician." www.ellensplace.net. Accessed: 12 October 2009.

McLain, Ruth G. *Little—and Mighty.* Colorado Crosscut. Arvada, CO: We Write of Colorado, 1975.

Miller, Jean. Personal Interview. 9 October 2009.

Mining Reporter. "The Yampa Coal Fields." Vol 50. 25 August 1904.

Thompsom, Mildred. Doc Susie Memories. Ts. Grand County Historical Museum.

Tucker, Edna. Interview. Ts. 17 October 1976. Grand County Historical Museum.

Willhite, Hattie. Interview. Ts. 19 October 1976. Grand County Historical Museum.

Zuckerman, Leo. "Fraser Residents Proud of Ice Box Title." *Rocky Mountain News.* 16 December 1951.

Zuckerman, Leo. "81-Year-Old Doc Susie is Fraser's Old Physician." *Rocky Mountain News.* 17 December 1951.

Index

Anderson, John, 4,5,6,7,8,9,13, 15, 16,17,18,49
Anderson, Minnie, 5,6,7,8,9,10,14,15
Anderson, Susan,
 childhood, 1-3
 death, 49
 education, 3-5, 8-10
 illness, 12, 20
 medical practice, vii, 13-14, 19, 23-25, 35-36, 38, 42, 44
 mother (Marya Pile Anderson), 1, 2, 11, 15
Anderson, William, 1, 2, 3, 6, 7-8, 9, 16

Barrymore, Ethel, 47
Blackwell, Elizabeth, 8, 10

Colorado General Hospital, vii
Cornell, Virginia, 50-51
Cripple Creek, Colorado, 7, 8, 12, 13, 14, 49

Denver, Colorado, 19,26, 31, 48, 49
Denver Post, 36, 40

Fraser, Colorado, vii, 20, 21, 22, 27, 30-31, 32, 33, 42, 43, 44, 47, 50

Grand County, Colorado, 27, 50
Great Depression, 42, 43
Greeley, Colorado, 19

Influenza Epidemic of 1918, 33-34

Lapham, Mary, 9, 14

Middle Park, 22, 27, 29, 33, 40, 44
Moffat, David, 26
Moffat Road, 20, 21, 26, 31, 33
Moffat Tunnel, 35,37, 39, 40
Morse code, 3, 4

Nevada Mills, Indiana, 1

Rollins Pass, 20, 31, 33, 35, 37, 39, 40

St. Catherine's Hospital, 10

Telegraph, 3
Thompson, Mildred, 43, 44, 46

University of Michigan, 8, 46

Warner, Cora and Charlie, 21
Wichita, Kansas, 2, 3, 5
Winter Park Ski Area, 45

Yampa coal fields, 31, 32

Acknowledgments

Without the help of the following people, I could not have completed this book. I am grateful for their time, efforts, and encouragement: Tim Nicklas and the staff at Grand County Historical Museum, Stephanie Miller at the Fraser Valley Library, Townsend Anderson at Historic Routt County, Mike Yurich at the Tracks and Trails Museum, Paul and Ellen Bonnifield, Ravay Snow, Jeanne Miller, Doris Baker, and especially Virginia Cornell.

About the Author

Lydia Griffin is the author of two children's picture books: *BeBa and the Curious Creature Catchers* and *Prunes and Rupe*, a story of friendship between a miner and his burro. Lydia is a graduate of Holderness School, Colorado College, and received her MFA from Spalding University. She enjoys teaching creative writing workshops to elementary and high school students. She has also taught college-level writing courses. She lives in the Rocky Mountains with her husband and dog.

Lydia is grateful to the courageous people who work in the medical profession, especially doctors like Susan Anderson who dedicate their lives to serving other people. To learn more about the author or to contact her, please visit her website at www.lydiagriffin.com.

More Now You Know Bios

Chipeta
1843 – 1924
ISBN 978-0-86541-091-6. $8.95

Mary Elitch Long
1856-1936
ISBN 978-0-86541-094-7. $8.95

John Denver
1943 – 1997
ISBN 978-086541-088-6. $8.95

Dottie Lamm
ISBN 978-086541-085-5. $8.95

Emily Griffith
1868-1947
ISBN 978-0-86541-077-0. $8.95

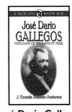
José Dario Gallegos
1830-1883
ISBN 978-0-86541-084-8. $8.95

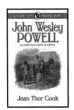
John Wesley Powell
1834-1902
ISBN 978-0-86541-080-0. $8.95

Justina Ford
1871-1952
ISBN 978-0-86541-074-9. $8.95

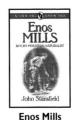
Enos Mills
1870-1922
ISBN 978-0-86541-072-5. $8.95

Martha Maxwell
1831-1881
ISBN 978-0-86541-075-6. $8.95

Molly Brown
1867-1932
ISBN 978-0-86541-081-7. $8.95

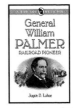
General William Palmer
1836-1909
ISBN 978-0-86541-092-3. $8.95

Bob Sakata
ISBN 978-0-86541-093-0. $8.95

Now You Know Bios are available at your local bookstore, by calling 888.570.2663, and online at www.FilterPressBooks.com